Even Buddhas Have Bad Days

Poems About Being Human

Written by Kate Quartermaine

Illustrated by Lisa Williams

Even Buddhas Have Bad Days

Poems About Being Human

Written by Kate Quartermaine
Illustrated by Lisa Williams

First published in 2023

ISBN: 978-1-7392804-0-6

TAUK
Publishing

For human beings — everywhere.

Contents

Musings

Fiddle De Dum

Oh, fiddle de dum and fiddle de dee
This world's an illusion
But it seems real to me.

Dear Reader

Dear reader, may I not offend
Upset is not what I intend
You disagree with what I write
Please do, that is your human right
Know your own truth, know your own mind
I only ask you, please be kind
To argue is not my intent
Just some support, encouragement
So please don't judge, find fault, or scorn
My truths from my experience born.

I'll not confess my years to you
That, for a lady, will not do
Suffice it tho' my right to say
That many times I've passed the way
Of anger, tasted fear and guilt
Wallowed in them if thou wilt
Trod the pathway of despair
Convinced myself that life's unfair
Judged and been judged in my turn
Let many bridges break and burn.

Yet somehow I have found a place
Where I can my own demons face
Found my heart, my truth, my home
Realised that I'm not alone
So if these verses can inspire
Give hope in circumstances dire
Comfort, amuse or stimulate
Int'resting thoughts and keen debate
Then I shall know I've laboured well
My very personal truth to tell.

A Poet's Dilemma

Shall I write poems dark and deep
Or pretty, full of lambs and sheep?
Shall I write poems deep and strong
Or bright and cheerful, not too long?
Shall I write poems that make us laugh
Or poems far too sad by half?

Or shall I write poems to inspire
To set the human soul on fire
To swell the heart in human chest
To help us know we're truly blessed
And shine a little chink of light
To help us in our human plight?

Hmmm…

Just Being Human

My Head

My head is such a busy place
I know I'd like to say
Serenity, it reigns supreme
But my thoughts get in the way.

There's a Rhino in My Garden

My life is like a garden, I try to tend it well
Create a place of happiness where I in peace may dwell.

I set my good intentions out, plant them in a row
Arranged in schemes of consequence and how well they might grow
I nourish and then water them, creating a fine show
Duly they begin to flower, their perfume fills the air
I smell content, accomplishment, see beauty everywhere.

But then a whole menagerie, escapees from some zoo
Invades my space, disturbs my peace, no matter what I do.

There's a monkey on my shoulder, he's trying to steal my joy
He comes to tease, destroy my ease, suggestion is his ploy
He'll whisper slyly in my ear, insinuate the worst
If I give him encouragement, he'll make me think I'm cursed.

There's a panther in the shrubbery, roaming round at large
His form is black, his thoughts are dark, he'd like to be in charge
His eye is keen for when I'm weak, he knows just where to pounce
It takes great strength to fight him off, and drains my every ounce.

The powerful hippopotamus, he really frightens me
Each time I plant my garden out, he comes along to see
He tramples my begonias and ruins all the grass
He'll wallow in my future dreams and wallow in my past.

And then there's this rhinoceros, the one that's mad as hell
He often just comes charging in, just when I cannot tell
He crashes through my rose bed, trashes those budding dreams
He doesn't want my happiness, at least that's how it seems.

I'm not quite sure how they get in, somehow I set them free
I know full well that they are just the darker part of me.

So then I have to start again, lay good intentions out
Plant my plans for happiness, weed out all the doubt
Reinforce my boundaries, make them good and stout
Affirm my resolution, make it clear and strong

Refuse to let the chaos win, know I've not gone wrong.
But next a soft spoke silky snake comes slithering along
Suggesting I should just give up, it's taking far too long
He sings a smooth and sinuous song, it almost lures me in
If I give up and walk away, I know that he will win.

Then comes the crow to bother me, his beak is sharp and keen
He worries at my confidence and picks at every dream
With beady eye, he'll ask me why, and is it really so?
Who am I to even try to make my garden grow?

One thing that is very clear, they have no care for me
They'll take my future happiness and rip it up with glee
They'll prod and taunt and tease and scorn and never let me
be
Until I own and somehow tame, this, my menagerie.

Me and Myself

Me and myself, we get on quite well
Well, sometimes we argue, on that I won't dwell
Me and myself, we work as a team
But sometimes we fall out; things are not as they seem.

I want to be tidy, with an organised house
Be a perfect housewife, mother and spouse
But the other me, well, she's not having that
She wants to be lazy and blousy and fat
Eat from the pan and lick clean the plate
Be messy and dirty and selfish and late
Drink lots of wine and shout at the kids
Make careless mistakes, then just tell massive fibs
Ignore all the housework and watch telly all day
And sometimes, I'm sorry, she just gets her way.

There She Is

There she is, my daughter, tiny, newly born
How fragile is her start in life
How deep this love I've sworn.

There she is, my daughter, school days passing by
I can't deny she's growing up
However hard I try.

There she is, my daughter, there for all to see
Stepping forward on life's stage
Proudly, nervously.

There she is, my daughter, cradling her own
How happy she is feeling now
How fast her life has flown.

There she is, my daughter, working busily
I hope her dreams are coming true
She means so much to me.

There she is, my daughter, with gently greying hair
Her age is bringing challenges
I wish that I was there.

There she is, my daughter, finally she's passed
I'm going down to welcome her
She's coming home at last.

Missing Sue

I grieve, my friend, for plans undone
Lost summer visits, summer fun
No more to go to Bilberry Wood
To talk to trees, or wish we could
Such happy times then, life was good.

No conversations on the phone
No Sue to ring when I'm alone
No more a sympathetic ear
To help when life seems grey and drear
Or when I'm tense and full of fear.

No more to shop and café hop
We couldn't know that this would stop.
No more to get dressed up to dine
Or just relax and savour time
Read a book, drink some wine.

We used to laugh so much we cried
But that all ended when you died
We didn't know your end would come
So soon, and leave so much undone
That friendship's thread would be unspun.

I grieve, my friend, for all that's lost
For friendship's love has dearly cost
My heart 

And Yet

The world counted and mourned its newly dead
And still the blackbird cocked his head
To listen for the worm.

And there is beauty yet.

The world counted and clapped its heroes new
While the season changed, as seasons do
Bud into early bloom.

The world counted and wept at its moneys lost
'Though nature did not count the cost
Nature thrived anew.

So much beauty yet.

Lockdown Lazy

Lockdown has made me quite lazy
Lockdown has done its darned best
To drag me down from a girl about town
To a slob of a blob in a vest.

We Only Went to Filey

Told by a young Yorkshire child

We only went to Filey
For our summer holiday
It don't take long to get to Filey
You can easy get there.

Amy went to Cornwall
For her summer holiday
There was sea and sand like we have here
But wow, what an exciting land
With magic pixies, dreamy cream teas
Eden's dome, exotic palm trees
It's just so very far away
The journey took a whole long day
In the car
To get there
Boring!

We only went to Filey
For our summer holiday
It don't take long
To get to Filey.
Anna went to France

On a camping holiday
There was sea and sand like we have here
Sun so hot she burnt, not tanned
She loved croissants and chocolate pan
And talking French, parlez, parlez.
But the journey took a whole long day
And a half
In the car
And she was sick
On the boat
Yuk!

We only went to Filey
It don't take long
It's not far.

Angela went to America
In a massive aeroplane
There was sea and sand like we have here
And magic magic Disneyland
She wants to go back there again
She liked it much much more than Spain
But she didn't like the jet lag
Or the time it took to get there
Or the times they had to stand and queue
Again and again

And again
Exhausting!

We only went to Filey
For our summer holiday
You can easy get there.
There was sea and sand, the beach was grand
We saw huge high cliffs and wild moorland
Stayed the week in a big chalet
And had a fantastic holiday.

The Early Train

At Crewe station in the summer, waiting for the early train
Summer lighted morning platform, glistening after morning rain
Muted people crowd the platform, time here is a waiting game
Quietly waiting the arrival, waiting for the early train.

Every traveller has their reason to rise bleary-eyed from bed
Catch the early train to London, planning for the day ahead
Business, family, shopping, culture, expectations to be fed
To London, London, they wait quietly, quietly waiting to be sped.

London's calling, London beckons, promising it will fulfil
For each their purpose, each their pleasure, all the London day until
Evening time comes, destination, hotel room or travel still
The evening train, the return journey, two more travelling hours to kill.

Has the spent day been successful, have the tourists had their fun?

Have the businesspeople prospered, contracts signed and business done?
Have the shoppers found their treasures or has disappointment come?
Were the planned reunions happy? Was London hot in summer sun?

But for now, they all are waiting, hopes are high despite the rain
There's much to come and much to play for, much to savour, much to gain
They're sure their journey won't be wasted, they won't be travelling south in vain
And so the early crowd stands patient, waiting for the early train.

Where Goes My Money?

Where goes my money, tripperty trip?
Slips through my fingers, slipperty slip
Clips through my bank account, clipperty clip
Fast as it comes, whipperty whip
It's come and it's gone again, slipperty slip
There goes my money, flipperty flip
Flipperty, flipperty, flipperty flip!

Credit Cards

Our credit cards entice us in
Have it all they seem to say
Buy it now, don't wait awhile
Having this will make you smile
You do know one day you must pay
But that dim future's far away.

Bright shiny bits of plastic
Just giving us the wink
Do it now, be Jack-the-lad
Paying the bill won't be that bad
Spend it now, don't even think
Buy that car, that dress, that drink.

They offer such an easy credit
You know one day you'll have to pay
But with this plastic spending power
Funds in your hand at any hour
Your better judgement's led astray
And you choose the easy way.

So you spend and spend again
Then you spend some more
But whilst on this happy spending spree
There's something you refuse to see
Forgetting universal law
Until the piper's at your door.

Well, you've had your good times now
But those bills won't go away
The deeds are done, the die is cast
Easy fortune now is past
You've had your fun, the piper's come
And now you've got to pay;
Not some far tomorrow but today.

Hindsight gives us easy wisdom
We may look back and rue the day
Temptation came, such easy gain
We let our credit take the strain
And our desires lead us astray
Because, one day, we have to pay.

The Happy Land of Might Have Been

In the happy land of Might Have Been
Where all the grass grows evergreen
How different now this life would seem
If we could live in Might Have Been.

Life would be easy, life would be sweet
Our expectations it would meet
We'd made good choices, errors few
Done all it was we needed to
We took our chances when they came
We lost the weight, we won the game
We backed the horse that won the race
We made our fortune, found our place
All of this, what could have been
In the happy land of Might Have Been.

To wish we lived there is not wise
In that direction torment lies
Focussing on what we lack
Will never bring those chances back

And with our minds, we cannot view
The futures those dreams took us to.

No matter, for the truth to tell
Here and now's where we must dwell
We'll never get to Might Have Been

That happy place will stay unseen
We must content ourselves instead
With where it is our paths have led.

Hyacinths

There are hyacinths on the hallway table
Carefully placed where they're able
To cheer the hall and scent the house
To lift my heart, myself to rouse
From winter with its closeting
To open, eager, coming spring.

New life, new growth, new starts, new me
I hope this coming year there'll be.

So…

As nature steadily awakes
I vow to do all that it takes
My inner challenges to face
And live life from a better place.

The Cherry Tree

I shall plant a cherry tree
In a blue pot on my balcony
A living sign for all to see
That I love you
But do you love me?

Please Like Me

For the playground of life

I really hope you like me
I need a friend that's new
With whom to share
Someone who's fair
And that friend could be you.

I really hope you'll like me
I need approval too
With your help, I may feel good
I may feel I will do.

I really hope you'll like me
I've made an effort too
I brushed my hair
Chose clothes with care
I think I hope I'll do.

I really hope you'll like me
And to help my wish come true
I'll say nice things and flatter you
And say that I like you.

And if you do not like me
My hurt I will not show
I'll stick my nose up in the air
Pretend that I don't really care
And say, I don't like you!

Hidden Hurts

We keep our hurts within us
Hidden, buried deep
We keep our hurts within us
And so our hearts do weep.

My Favourite Subject

There's a subject that I find enthralling
When I am out and about
Mixing with friends and acquaintances
That holds my attention, no doubt
It's a theme I can talk on for ages
With sparkle and great repartee
It's me, I'm my favourite subject
My favourite subject is me
On the subject of me, I'm an expert
Oh, I do know a lot about me.

Now, when we are in conversation
There are ways you can help me feel good
And then I will find that I like you
And that I actually could
Be interested in what you are doing
In your life, but then you must see
That I really prefer my own subject
My favourite subject is me
I can talk on this subject for ages
I do like to talk about me.

I'm quite happy to talk about you for a while
I'll pay full attention, I'll nod and I'll smile
I'll be sympathetic, condole if you're sad
I'll laugh at your jokes, even when bad
But then you must pay me attention
That's something you really must do
For I am my favourite subject
That's ME, I am sorry, not you.

House of Thorns

We've built a house of thorns, my dear
This house of you and I
We've built a house of hurts, my dear
And now we both do cry.

You know there's no togetherness
We never do agree
I know that you're no more the one
Who brings content to me.

You know that there is no respect
Between the two of us
I know that love left long ago
Joy withering to dust.

You know my ways so well by now
Just how and when to wound
I know your secret wretchedness
And so our house is doomed.

You know just how to punish me
When to withhold your heart
I know just how to spoil your dreams
By ripping them apart.

So let's pull down this house of thorns
The house of you and me
Each build a new one for themselves
Where peace and comfort be.

A Dieter's Lament

I've decided I really must lose weight
And in order to try to do that
I'll need to adopt certain strategies
That could help me lose this excess fat.

I know that I should try to diet
Though the word itself makes my heart sink
All of my past experiences say
Just be careful with this, first, please think.
Remember how hard you have found it
To lose weight and then keep that weight off
You know it's so easy to weaken
And then you just scoff and you scoff.

I know that it could be quite helpful
To exercise more to burn fat
I should go to the gym or go running
But there's no time for any of that
You see, life is really quite busy
I just can't do whatever I like
I have so many other commitments
I can't just take off for a hike.

I could start to use affirmations
I'll affirm I am thin and not fat
But the trouble with this affirmation
Is most of me doesn't think that
And certainly all of my trousers
Will now ascertain to the fact
That my waistline is gradually spreading
And I really do know I must act
To halt this insidious expansion
This monstrous expansion of fat.

In some parts my body's quite dimpled
I don't think that's how it should be
Smooth, soft, without dimple or wrinkle
Is really what I'd like to see
But cellulite's just not forgiving
It can strike even slim models down
So now I must detox and diet
And hope that some fat turns to brown.

Then, when I've decided to diet
Which diet should I adopt?
There's keto, low fat or low calorie
Or fasting when mealtimes are stopped
Paleo, raw food, low glycaemic ?
Just eat cabbage soup, which I hate

Oh, which is the way to go forward?
Which diet will help me lose weight?

In the past I have tried many diets
On some of them I have done well
Yet somehow, I can't keep that weight off
It's distressing; I try not to dwell
On how good it would feel to be slimmer
To have lost that strong urge to rebel
Eat those beautiful biscuits and chocolates
On how good it would be to just quell
Those ravenous cravings and munchings
Because there lies my own pudgy hell.

Maybe I could talk to my fat cells
They're just trying to look after me
Preparing for times of starvation
Survival is their gift, you see
But I wish I could alter their programme
So my burgeoning fat cells then know
In this life there's no risk of starvation
And I just do not need them to grow.

I am told stress can be a big factor
Those hormones can play a large part
So I now need to balance my lifestyle
Relax, not get stressed for a star

And I'll choose to look after my body
Not view it with loathing and hate
Accept that it may not be perfect
Accept, for now, this excess weight.
I'll choose to let go of the struggle
I'll choose to love all parts of me
I'll try not to stuff down those feelings
Of total inadequacy
I'll accept that I have imperfections
Accept them with love, not resist
For love is the very best diet
And what we resist will persist
There's the twist
Love's the best diet there is.

This Body

This body has been well-lived in
It's got its lumps and bumps
This body's been around the block
And it's sure got its grumps.

This body's seen some action
We've really had some fun
This body's had some hard times too
When all is said and done.

This body's quite amazing
I could fault its design
But then, without its wobbly bits
It wouldn't feel like mine.

This body's getting older now
I'd like to say mature
Ripe and fruity, rich and full
I wish I could say pure.

This body's got an ending
My life will end one day
I know it's not forever
That I get to live and play.

But while I've got this body
And 'tho it's not perfect
I'll cherish it with gratitude
And treat it with respect.

The Saga of a Reformed Vegetarian

Kate, now red in tooth and claw
Is vegetarian no more.

A veggie from a quite young age
She used to fly into a rage
When people said that meat was good
For her, and that she really should
Partake of beast and fowl and fish
Because she didn't really wish
To eat the cow with languid looks
The playful lamb from storybooks
The rooting pig, the clucking hen
The fish that swim and others, when
Such good alternatives were there
Pulses, nuts and suchlike fare
And these could be so tasty too
In nut roasts, pies or lentil stew.

So flesh she swore she would not eat
Indeed, this seemed an easy feat
Righteously she ate her nuts

Content for years, then came the 'buts'
An uneasy sense all was not well
But what was wrong, she couldn't tell
A tiredness and a slight malaise
Began to blight her nights and days.

And then she heard her body cry:
I'll tell you the reason why
There's something wrong with what you eat
It's not complete, I need some meat
I've got to say, I've had enough
Of tofu, beans and veggie stuff
Roots are fine, and some leaves too
But meatless meals, they just won't do
They leave me hungry, craving food
And all this does not do me good
You must let go your high ideal
To not eat flesh, and just get real.

Our ancestors from ancient times
Inhabited these northern climes
They hunted, gathered and survived
By eating flesh, those humans thrived
And that is how this your body's wired
It's no wonder that you're feeling tired
What makes you think you can forget

Your genes, and just use intellect
To plan your meals and so ignore
My need to be a carnivore?
As your body, again, I'll say
That I just wasn't made that way.

Now, if you came from southern climes
And had done so since ancient times
Too much meat would not be good
In fact, those people really should
Be moderate in flesh intake
For their health and bodies' sake
And those people really could
Be vegetarian if they would.

But you're not them, and so you see
You really must listen to me
I'll tell you when you've got it right
'Cos basically, you'll feel quite bright
Your energy will feel renewed
Your body's strength restored, refuelled
Your head will be clear, emotions stable
And for several hours you will be able
To not think of food or crave a snack
'Cos you'll be content, there'll be no lack
Of all the things this body needs

To fuel itself and do your deeds
And when it's time to eat once more
And when your trust in me is sure
I'll tell you what I need to eat
And that certainly includes some meat
Please think upon this if you're able
In future when you come to table.

So let's thank the sheep, the hen, the cow
And other creatures that even now
Surrender life to humankind
And trust that their heaven they'll find
Where they can be in quiet content
Their destiny, for which they're meant
But while they're here, in our control
Remember, creatures too have soul
And their lives deserve respect
Not misuse or cruel neglect
Let's try to help human beings see
The gift they give to you and me.

Her body now had had its say
And this, for Kate, had changed the way
She thought about the food she ate
And animals, what is their fate?
She vowed at once to listen to

Her body, 'cos she knew it knew
Just what was right for her to eat
And that certainly included meat
With this she now made her peace
Which brought about a great release.

So Kate, now red in tooth and claw
Is vegetarian no more.

Heron

Sharp of beak and sharp of eye
Slowly, surely, stalking by,
The heron seeks his watery prey
Each and every watery day.

In the shallows, small fish thrive
Slim and slick, swift and lithe
Darting quick from side to side
Glinting scales in silver tide.

Self-contained and statue still
With staring eye and stabbing bill
The heron waits with patient will
His feast to come, his prey to kill.

Suddenly, the pounce, the strike
Small fish scatter all alike
Save the one impaled and doomed
To be now swallowed and consumed.

Thus sustained, the heron thrives
Eating little fishy lives
His life dependent on this kill
Survival on his fishing skill.

Many little fish live lives
But few to adulthood survive.
It seems that this is nature's way
Some will be hunters, some the prey.

A Difficult Birthday

Forty was a doddle
Fifty was a breeze
I waltzed into my sixties
With confidence and ease
But seventy's proving difficult
It's becoming very clear
How quickly time is passing by
Each day, each week, each year.

I do get passing compliments
I feel good for my age
But inside me, slowly building
Is an existential rage
Why, oh, why is life so short?
I've hardly started yet
There's still so much I want to do
But now I can't forget
That time is quickly passing by
The time that I've got left
I'm just getting the hang of life
But now I feel bereft.

It's said these are our golden years
And that it might be best
To lead a gentler way of life
Relax and take more rest
For that, I'm just not ready
The flame within burns strong
There's passion from the heart of me
A wish life will be long.

So I'm calling these my bonus years
I hope to use them well
How many of them have I left?
That I cannot tell.

Seventy

With acknowledgement to Wendy Cope's poem about her cat.

I will be 70 years old next Saturday
But I have decided
Not to make
A big thing
Of
It.

Hard Work

I'm making hard work of my life at the moment
This living thing's getting me down
The smile on my face is wearing quite thin
And becoming replaced by a frown.

I'm finding it all just a bit much
My mood is depressingly low
It's all just become a big burden
Full of hard work and struggle and so

I work and I struggle and worry
And then I just worry some more
The whole world seems in such a hurry
I feel stressed right down to my core.

I know that I want to be happy
I know I don't want to be stressed
I know that I do want contentment
Or is that just for those who've been blessed?

I know I don't want to be fearful
For fear, I know, gets in the way
I try to find my inner courage
And keep all those dark thoughts at bay.

I do try to make my life better
I read all the right books, you know
I work hard on my self-approval
But progress is terribly slow.

I know that this life can be heaven
I know that this life can be hell
How on earth do I make the right choices?
How on earth can I learn to choose well?

They say there are angels and helpers
To guide human beings on our way
All we need do is just ask them
All we need do is just pray.

So I'll pray that my guides and my angels
Will help me choose well and choose right
Help me fulfil my soul's purpose
Help me find my inner light.

And I'll thank them for what I am given
For this life is a gift, I've no doubt
Though part of me still wonders sometimes
What is it all really about?

Idiosyncrasies

Idiosyncrasies, I've got a few
And some I don't know about
How about you?

Human Being

Joy, a Definition

My soul's purpose and I are one.

Even Buddhas Have Bad Days

My hair's a mess, my halo's slipped
And I'm feeling a little bit fraught
Struggling to enjoy today
In the way that I think that I ought
I really am quite out of sorts
In an unsettling kind of way
I simply can't seem to get on with things
Today is just not a good day.

But I think even Buddhas have bad days
I'm sure saints have their problems too
Sometimes this life's just not easy
And it's OK for me and for you
To surrender the struggle for one day
Acknowledge we're not at our best
Be kind to ourselves, make it easy
Decide that today we will rest.

So, I'll do things that I really need to
I will do all those things that I can
But then I'll just do what I want to
And trust in the infinite plan.

There's an Angel at My Shoulder

There's an angel at my shoulder
There's an angel by my side
Watching, waiting patiently
Trying to be my guide.

Does he wonder as he watches
Lord, what's she up to now
Do all those silly things I do
Leave furrows in his brow?
Because I know I'm not an angel
I'm certainly no saint
I'm sure some things I get up to
Could make an angel faint.

Or does he just not see them
Or seeing, he doesn't mind?
He knows I'm just being human
And there's no fault to find.

There's an angel at my shoulder
Standing very near
He's trying to guide my footsteps
He'll whisper in my ear

Sometimes I cannot hear him
Sometimes I could, but don't
Sometimes I hear his message clear
Sometimes I sulk and won't.

But does he then give up on me
Like many people would
Decide that he has had enough
Of not doing any good?

He won't, for he's my angel
He's standing there right now
To guide me is his purpose
To help me is his vow
So, please, angel at my shoulder
Step forward, take a bow.

POSTSCRIPT
By the way, in case you're wondering
I've called my angel he
Although angels have no gender
Neither he nor she
Angels come from realms beyond
Our own duality
I'm just a little lazy
And it's easier for me.

Soul Rush

There's glory in this human form, such bliss, such joy, O to be
born
To come into this world and yet to rise above, not to forget
Our own divine true origin. If you could see what this could
mean
Know what a joy this life can be, to know your own divinity
To know that we can really see, what lies in you, what lies in
me.

We get ensnared by worldly things, concerns and cares and
worryings
But when we let our hearts fly free, then what beauty we can
see
Thus lifted up we can proceed and travel where our paths
may lead
Through lessons easy, lessons sweet, lessons hard, each we
can meet
And greet them with a knowing smile, invite them in to stay a
while.

To teach us true, to teach us well, to tell us all they have to tell
And when at last we've done enough, we've learnt our
lessons, sweet and tough

To say goodbye then to the learning, to answer our heart's inner yearning
To leave this schoolroom, leave this form, go back to where our souls were born
Back to where our souls were born

Transfigured

Sometimes in my daily round
I seem to stand on hallowed ground
And view a common scene of day
Transfigured in some magic way
A scene transfused with peace and light
A peace so deep, a light so bright
So beautiful, it seems to me
That this must be what angels see.

Which then leads me to surmise
This blessed state must be life's prize
And men and women will be blind
Until this happy truth they find
Until they open inner eyes
And trust their hearts to make them wise.

Sometimes Found

Somehow I have sometimes found
A doorway to another realm
Where creatures mythical abound
So real to see, so real to me
Reality becomes unsound
I know they're there 'though few can see
This mystical reality
No pretty painted imagery
But vibrant, real as you or me
These hidden realms where fairies be.

So now I see a task ahead
To share what I have seen
To put aside my fear and dread
And clearly state my truth instead
How wonderful it then would be
If others accept graciously
This magical reality
That there are realms where fairies be.

Who Am I?

I am just a little soul trying to find the light
I am just a little soul trying to fight my fight
I am just a little soul trying to do what's right
I am just a little soul trying with all my might.

I am just a little soul learning to be free
I am just a little soul learning how to be
I am just a little soul learning how to see
I am just a little soul; I'm only me.

Oh, I am just a little soul, but I shine so bright
I am just a little soul, but I'm full of light
I am just a little soul, but I'm quite a sight
I'm not just a little soul, I hadn't realised quite,

That I'm not just a little soul, there's something I now see
I'm not just a little soul, a leaf upon the tree
I'm not just a little soul, I've looked inside of me
I see I'm part of everything, and everything is me.

I Was There

I was there
Not close, you understand
Not one of the inner circle
I was never that
But I was there
One of the faces in the crowd
One of those who came to listen
And understood.

Yes, I was there
Just one of the faces in the crowd
But I am content
I was there.

The Wave, The Leopard and The Rainbow

Can a wave depart the ocean
The leopard shed a single spot
Can a rainbow lose its colours
Or humans lose what's just forgot?

We can't deny our higher nature
Although so many of us try,
Within us is the path to glory
And all will come there by and by.

Trying to Be the Lotus

Trying to be the lotus
Trying to find the light
Roots in muddy waters
Heart at Heaven's height.

Trying to be the lotus
Trying to still my mind
Rise above the tumult
Serenity to find.

Trying to be the lotus
Trying to be awake
Asking for some guidance
A higher path to take.

Trying to be the lotus
Trying to come from love
Hoping for detachment
And strength to rise above.

Trying to be the lotus
Trying to meditate
Aiming for enlightenment
To gain that blessed state.

Trying to be the lotus
Trying to look within
Find my light and let it shine
Let my true heart win

The lotus is used as a symbol of detachment in many Eastern traditions. The lotus plant has its roots in the muddy bottom of the lake, while its beautiful blooms sit serenely on the surface in the light.

The Art of Contemplation

With a nod to Jane Austen

The art of contemplation
It's sad to say, but true
By and large escapes me now
There's just so much to do
There's the shopping and the cooking
And all the housework too
There's kids to raise and every day
Much must be done anew.

The art of contemplation
That really does sound good
I'd love to have a crack at it
And if I could, I would
But you see, I'm very busy
I'd like to try, it's true
But what with work and other things
Well, what's a girl to do?

The art of contemplation
The art of feeling good
About myself, about the world
I know I wish I could

Maybe I'll have a go at it
Before I go to bed
But then maybe I'll be too tired
And go to sleep instead.

The art of contemplation
Is it really true?
I could find my own inner peace
It's there for me and you?
I know, I'll get up early
Somehow I'll find the time
I'll sit me down and turn within
Let go of me and mine.

Dear reader, wow, I've done it
I have, I've found the time
I tweaked my busy schedule
And reader, 'tis divine.

Moments

Alone, in quieter moments
In the spaces between time
I can sometimes glimpse a reason
See a truth that's more than mine.

A Suggestion as to How You Could Proceed

Begin by consulting your own heart
As to where you are going and why
It will tell you for what you are searching
And which likely paths you could try

Free it to follow its yearning
Let it lead, it will guide you full well
For it knows you and loves you
Does not harshly judge you
And your own inner truth it will tell.

Try to listen, 'midst all of life's clamour
To its gentle but insistent call
For it is your own wisdom
Your courage and freedom
Your own song, your purpose, your all.

How to Hear Your Heart Sing

If you want to hear your heart sing
You must be still, very still
And small, very small
And quiet.

And when it comes
And sings
You will know
That this is what you've always wanted.

I Shall Give My Worries to the Angels

I shall give my worries to the angels
My burdens and my fears
For they will take good care of them
And wipe away my tears.
Although I cannot see them yet
I know they're there for me
Watching, waiting patiently
For the time when I can see.

I shall give my worries to the angels
It's very simply done

Just ask for help and they will hear
Just call and they will come.

Their loving care will comfort me
With them I will converse
We'll talk of life and reasons why
My fretting soul they'll nurse.

I shall give my worries to the angels
I'll let go angst and pain
Say goodbye to suffering
Be happy once again.

My deepest hurts they'll help me heal
My heart will find release
With guiding love they'll help me see
How I may find my peace.

Help Me Please

Help me as I live my life please
Help me as I go along
I shall need your loving care, Lord
Then by your grace I can be strong.

Help me when I start to stumble
And my strength begins to fail
Your love will aid me if I falter
Your strength support me when I'm frail.

Help me if I sometimes stumble
And my strength begins to fail
With your help I will not falter
Your strength will be there when I'm frail.

Help me please when I am worried
Cares and burdens weigh me down
Your love will make my burdens lighter
Your smile will smooth away my frown.

Help me please when I am tempted
Away from what is dear to me

Show me what I really want, then
Show me what I need to see.

Help me please if grief o'erwhelms me
And I, despairing, lose my way
Help me find the hope inside me
Know you're with me come what may.

Help me please when I anger
And gall makes mine a bitter cup
Fill my heart to overflowing
With sweet love for me to sup.

Help me please when I am lonely
Lacking human company
Let me know you're close beside then
Let me know you're there for me.

Help me please when I feel envy
Of others who have more than me
Help me see all I've been given
Show me how to become free.

Help me please if I am fearful
Afraid of what might come to pass
Help me live my life with courage
And face my fears, that's what I ask.

Help me if my body pains me
And becomes too burdensome
Help me know this too will pass, Lord
Help me know relief will come.

Help me when I think I've failed, Lord
Give me strength to carry on
Help me not let go my effort
Help make sure my work is done.

I thank you for I know you'll help me
As I live my life each day
Your love and grace will be there for me
Your guiding light will show my way.

Now

Now is my moment, now is my hour
Now is for acting, now's in my power
Now does my heartbeat, now's my soul's chance
Now is for stepping into this life's dance.

Now is for doing when all deeds are done
Now is the moment each battle is won
Now is important, not future, nor past
Now's for deciding how my fate is cast.

Now is my present, now is for me
Now is the place where I can be free
Now is the moment when I sing my song
Now is for choosing to be weak or strong.

Now could be my heaven or could be my hell
Now's for creating the place where I dwell
Now is my treasure trove, now is my joy
The gift of this moment I will not destroy.

Never Give Up

Never give up and let your dreams go
Think the effort's not worth it, you've nothing to show
Don't be disheartened and throw in the towel
Let dreams that you've cherished turn bitter and foul.

Never give up when your plans don't work out
Don't surrender defeated or concede to self-doubt
Just take a step backwards, change and adjust
Then go on forward, go forward you must.

Never give up, though the path that you seek
May sometimes feel lonely and terribly steep
Don't be discouraged when the journey seems slow
Be brave and go places where others don't go.

Never give up though you know you've gone wrong
Life is for learning and lessons are long
Don't say it's all over, with this you are done
There's plenty to play for, it's time to move on.

Never give up until your last breath
For this path continues right up to your death
Live life your own way, get up when you fall
Failure's not failure when you've given your all.

Wise Words

The world clamours loud with a rumble and drum
Its glamour invites us and forward we come
To join in the dance, the play that's begun
And escape from its rhythms is granted to none.
Our life is a gift that we cannot refuse
It's for us to value or ours to misuse
Given with love, by a greater design
What is its reason our souls will divine

We can live here with dignity, purpose, and grace
Despite all the tumult, chaos and pace
If, in the rush, we are willing to pause
Seek our souls' purpose and heed divine laws
We may question the why, the where or the how
What we do know is the moment called now
The past is behind us, we cannot change that
Tomorrow's not here yet, the future's not fact
Our power's in this moment, each moment's the one
We're shaping our fate and the life that's to come.

We all have our talents, some many, some few
To help us accomplish what we're here to do.
Fashion your life with the gifts that are yours

Know you do have a reason, purpose and cause
We come here to learn, experience and grow
Come from great love, that great love to know
As love is our reason, our purpose and source
This love will sustain us throughout our life's course.

Hark not to the thought you're unworthy of love
We are our worst critic, we are our own judge
No human is perfect, you know this is true
Don't aim for perfection, be happy being you
In this vast game of life, play your own little part
And you'll not go far wrong when you follow your heart.
Cherish your body, we only get one
It's yours to inhabit 'till this life is done
Respect all its seasons, pay heed to its needs
For you need its support in all of your deeds.

Be wise in your choices, for choice is your right
Know when it's your battle and when not to fight
Learn from mistakes, for mistakes you will make
Life is for learning, the lessons you take
Accept when you falter, accept when you lose
To learn from experience is your path to choose
Don't blame other people, or God, or blind chance
Just pick yourself up and re-join the dance
Life's precious prizes are lessons you've learnt

And there's no prize worth more than a prize that's well earnt.

Once you've made your effort, once you've cast your die
When you think it's too late, or you're too tired to try
Be humble, accepting, welcome your fate
For all's never lost and it's never too late.
Let fate then take over, let destiny come
Let your will be the will of the infinite one.
Then when the time comes, be gracious with death
For the journey continues beyond your last breath
When the web of your weaving, all you've thought and done
Will shine in your soul and the light you've become.

Being Mortal

I Know You Well

I know you well, Beloved
I know all that you do
Behind the mask you show the world
I know who's really you.

I love you so, Beloved
And I wait patiently
For the day that you are ready
To come back home to me.

I trust you too, Beloved
I trust one day you'll see
That I am at the heart of you
And you are part of me.

I sent you on a journey
Ranging far and wide
But though I sent you far away
I never left your side.

So turn your footsteps homeward
Listen to the call
We will be reunited
I will not let you fall.

The Journey Home

There's a journey that we all must take
The one that takes us home
Back to the place where we come from
And all must leave alone.

Some people find it easy
A blessing and release
They're happy to go home again
To go and find their peace.

Some people find it difficult
It's not so easy done
They've guilt and fear of punishment
This journey they will shun.

For some, it's hard to find the way
They do not know it's there
Denial, doubt and ignorance
Will keep them unaware.

Some people do not want to go
They've liked it too much here
Attachments to the lives they've led
Can bind them to this sphere.

Sometimes our own beloved ones
Just cannot let us be
Their need to keep us close to them
Will hinder our flying free.

So when it's time for you to go
To take that journey home
Remember, it's where you come from
Know you won't be alone.

Angels, guides and helpers wait
To assist you on your way,
All you do is ask for help
All you do is pray.

Fear not judgement, fear not loss
Fear not more worldly pain
Step forward to the guiding light
And you'll be home again.

I Have Gone On

Do not grieve for me
Do not be sad that I am no longer there
I have simply gone on.
Why should I stay when my time is done?

I may not have been with you long
But it was long enough for us to be together
If only for a little while
And long enough for us to love
If only for a little while.

Time has no meaning for love
Now that we have loved
Our love will always be there.

The bloom of real love never dies
It becomes instead a beautiful brushstroke
In the book of time.

Do not grieve for me.

Too Busy to Die

HUMAN BEING

Death's come calling round my way
But I'm far too busy to die today
I've much to do, I need to stay
Begone Death, begone I say
I'm far too busy to die today.

DEATH

I gave you threescore years and ten
The allotted span for mortal men
When you begged for more, another ten
I think this was a fair bargain
And yet you ask and ask again.

But Death, I'm just not ready yet
To leave this life without regret

I need more time, so I can get
My life in order, clear my debt
And then I'll leave with no upset.

I'm sorry but this is the time
It's plain in your soul's own timeline
With this plan you must align
The glass is empty, gone life's wine
Now is the end of this lifetime.

But Death, just give me one more spring
Please Death, let this be my choosing
A little time to keep living
To savour life, to savour being
One summer more before leaving.

That you know I cannot do
To your souls plan we must stay true
All was agreed, and your soul knew
That this last time your life was due
To end, and death must now ensue.

I cannot go, I've too much fear
Of losing all that I hold dear
And now you've come so very near
I fear a judgement, bleak and drear

I cannot see the pathway clear.

I see you think you're all alone
You do not know you're coming home
There's no more need this earth to roam
Why stay with all your lessons done?
Love is calling you, now come.
With one last easy outward breath
Now pass the portal into death
Love is coming, it won't take long
For you to find where you belong.

Remember the Soldier

Remember the soldier who fought for the cause
Whose life was surrendered with barely a pause
To ask was it worthy, ask was it right
To take the Kings shilling and enter the fight
Who thought there was glory in the deeds he would do
How soon did he realise this just wasn't true?

Remember the soldier who went off to war
Did he curse all the generals once he wondered what for?
Did he see that this glory was rotten right through
That war makes us do things no human should do?
Was he bitter and angry when he realised they'd lied?
Or stoic and brave while he secretly cried?

Remember the soldier who left wife and child
Were his last moments peaceful, or tortured and wild?
Did he cry for his mother when the pain got too much?
Did he beg for his sweetheart, her comforting touch?
Did his soul go to Heaven, did his soul go to Hell?
Or is there some other place he's gone to dwell?

Remember the soldier, remember him well.

The imagined soldier here is from the First World War, and "Taking the King's shilling" is a historical term that means enlisting, making a binding commitment to enlist in the British Army or Royal Navy.

On the Refugee Road

Europe 1940

No, no, no, I don't want this
Please, please, not this
I don't want to be here.

Noise screaming
Planes screeching, screeching, wailing, wailing
I don't want this, not this, here
Cowering. Terrified.
Body scrunched
Waiting.

I don't want this

Please, please, please
Let me not be here
Let them pass.
Earth, swallow me, save me
So I am not here, not now
Not this hell
Not here, not now.

Please, please, let it not be me
The devil planes and bombs
Seek
Screeching, screeching, screaming, wailing

Everywhere

Inside my head

Please, please
Let it be somewhere else
Someone else they find
Not here, not me
Not now
Please, please, please.

Waiting

Thunder bursting, head burning

Silent. Still
Distant screeching
Leaving
Sound receding
So quiet.

I'm not there

But where?

I'm not there

I am here

I am me, still me

Oh blessed, blessed, blessed me

The nightmare has passed over

And left me

Still me, I'm still me.

Peace be

Is that a light ahead?

Mary Evans

THE LAMENT

Mary Evans, Mary Evans
Young and fresh, not yet sixteen
Naïve and wishful, Mary Evans
Such a short, hard life it's been
Mary, late of Bangor Parish
How little of the world you'd seen

Mary, youthful Mary Evans
Not much wrong with you at all
Easy led, perhaps too trusting
Shyly smiling 'neath your shawl
Yet folk looked and harshly judged you
Punished you and watched you fall.

Mary, dear lost Mary Evans
How little of the world you'd seen.
Did he say that you were pretty?
And you, so very fresh and green
Believed it when he said he loved you
Betrayed, abandoned, just fifteen.

Oh, Mary, Mary, Mary Evans
Not much wrong with you at all
He deceived you with his promise
Walked away and watched you fall.
Scorned, rejected Mary Evans
Swaddled babe beneath your shawl.

Mary, frightened, Mary Evans
Condemned by all society
Humiliated, shamed, found guilty
Until death came to set you free
Yet fear of facing Hell's damnation
Left you lost, in purgatory.

MARY'S PLEA

Is someone there, Sir, can you help me?
Is that a friendly light I see?
Angel, spirit, hear my calling
Stranger, please, whoever you be
Look on me and treat me kindly
Is there a place for such as me?
I carry with me such a burden
Guilt and shame for all to see
Is there hope for one so wretched?
Could I, so very low, be free?
Angel, spirit, hear my calling

Stranger, please be kind to me
May one like me receive God's blessing?
Can God love one so shamed as me?

THE RESPONSE

Of course, of course, beloved Mary
Step up, step forward to the light,
You always have been loved and cared for
You are precious in our sight
Let go your burdens, you are free now
We have released you from your plight
Fear no more, for you are safe now
Know that all is made aright.

This poem is about a time when being pregnant and unmarried was considered extremely shameful, even a mortal sin, as it still is in many parts of the world. Generations of young girls and women have been humiliated and made to suffer for this, often with tragic consequences.

Mrs Jones

Mrs Jones went up to Heaven
Dressed all in her Sunday best
Hat secured with shiny hat pins
Handbag clutched against her chest.

Peter himself came to meet her
Met her at the pearly gates
Opened them and bade her enter
Come within, no need to wait.

In she walked, no hesitation
Firm her stride and set her face
Told him, *I've the right to be here*
I know that I have earned my place.

In Jesus I'm a true believer
To his kingdom I've now come
You keep out those non-believers
Those blasphemers we must shun.

Peter smiled at her and nodded
You may have what you expect
Here's your heaven, here your people
Come on in and join your sect.

Mrs Jones was very happy
I knew that I was right, she said
I knew that I would be rewarded
True believers are, once dead.

At first she really felt content there
People that she recognised
Greeted her and helped her settle
She truly felt she'd gained her prize

But one day, she started wondering
These thoughts gave her cause for doubt
Life here seems a little boring
What's my heaven all about?

If this is Heaven, where's the glory?
Where's the joy and where's the bliss?
Why is it my heart's not singing?
Something seems to be amiss.

Straight in came Peter with his angels
As if they had been listening
Waiting for the perfect moment
To tell her what she was missing.

We can answer now you've questioned
Here is not what Heaven is
This 'paradise' is just your construct
You've limited yourself to this.

Reality is so much greater
Than this place you've envisaged
Your true nature you've forgotten
And built yourself a pretty cage.

Human souls all come from one source
Truth's the same for everyone
Every human being is equal
There is no one we may shun.

Everyone creates their heaven
Everyone creates their hell
We build them with our expectations
And within them, we then dwell.

Until the moment that we question
Is this supposition right?
Start our hearts investigation
And see things in a different light.

On Dying

Why are you so afraid of dying
Dear beloved little one?
Do you not know that you'll come homewards
Back to us, where you belong?

Do you not know that we are waiting
Here to welcome you back home?
With much joy and celebration
To be united with the one?

Are you afraid of retribution
For some things you may have done?
Worry not my dear beloved
Love is where we all come from.

Are you afraid that you will vanish
Dissolved into eternity?
The real you can never vanish
It lives in you, it lives in me.

Surrender all that you have strived for
Let go all your fear and pain
Hold not on to acquisitions
Hold not on to worldly chains.

Let your spirit free to fly now
Towards the truth, towards the light
We, who love you, are rejoicing
As your mortal soul takes flight.

We will welcome you back home now
Shed your bonds and become free
Return to join us in the dance here
The dance that is eternity.

So, rest in peace now, my beloved
Rest easy as you breathe your last
Love will come to take you homewards
Peace you will find that's unsurpassed.

Gently

Gently, gently, come to peace now
Come to peace, no need for fright
Dearest one, do not be scared now
Your soul's weary, and near ready
To come back home, back to the light.

Softly, softly, now come forward
Feel the calling, feel the power
Feel the love that draws you onward
T'wards this most important moment
This destined time, this sacred hour.

Leave friends and family behind here
Earth's desires and business too
Time to move on, you are done here
None may follow, only you may
Take this journey, only you.

Let go all your pain and suffering
Lightly leave this life behind
Love will greet you, everlasting
Peace and beauty you will find.

Divine Being and Sacred Conversations

I Am the Song

I am the song that your life is now singing
I am the journey you take on life's path
I am the wayside, the road and the traveller
I am your home, your very own hearth

I am the story your life is now telling
I am the pathway leading you on
I am your wisdom, your guide and your tutor
I am the light guiding you home.

I am the meek, the mild and the lowly
I am the bold, the brave and the true
I am the essence of light now unveiling
I am incarnate, residing in you.

I am pure nature in all things unfolding
I am the template from which you all grew
I am the mystery, the knowledge inside you
I am the hidden you thought that you knew.

I am your story unfolding in time now
I am the record you make as you pass
I am the ending that all stories come to
I will be there when your breath is your last.

I am the glory within you to worship
I am the wisdom steering you true
I will be with you for ever and ever
For I am the power that gives life to you

I Got the Joke

Hi God, I got the joke, I got the joke today
Your love is here, so very near, it's just a breath away
Hidden there inside of us, like all the sages say
Yes, God, I got the joke, I got the joke today.

Hi God, I really got the joke, I got your joke today
You're everywhere and everything, it's all your divine play
I am all, all is me, that's all that I can say
Yes, God, I know I've got your joke, I've seen your divine play.

Hi God, I got the joke, I got your joke today
Love is all, all is love, and love will have its way
Oh yes, I really got the joke, I got your joke today
And God, I really love your joke, I love this joke, your play.

So God, now that I've got the joke, now I can see your play
In this state of sweet enlightenment, I pray that I may stay.

Humble

I really am ever so humble
But inside, I'm glorious and vast
I hope that on pride I don't stumble
As I think I have done in the past.

I really am ever so humble
But within me is so huge and vast
I hope I fulfil my life's purpose
As I play out the role I am cast.

I really am ever so humble
But so very glorious too
Now what do I do with this knowledge
That what's within me is in you?

Glory

Come sweet love, come great compassion
Come peace, release and banish shame
All the hurts we humans fashion
Bless them please, and ease our pain.

Come sweet breath, come deep rejoicing
Come joy, come song, come celebrate
This great love grows like wine maturing
Heady healing draughts of grace.

If people could just glimpse this glory
If they could only see this light
Then each could read their own soul's story
And know that all is made aright.

This Little Body

HUMAN BEING, QUESTIONING
Can this little body hold
A light so big, a truth so bold?
And this shining spirit be
Housed in one so small as me
And can this little human soul
Be really part of that great whole?

And may this fragile human heart
Know that great love of which it's part
And these hopeful eyes of mine
Behold the inner truth divine
And may this breath, this life, this gift
This humble human being uplift
And my imperfect human love
Be honoured in the realms above?

THE RESPONSE
Your very being's designed to hold
This light so big, this truth so bold
And your human form was born
To know this love to which you're drawn.
Rest easy, all these gifts will come
Before your little soul is done.

I Will Come

Beloved one
Do not worry
I will come.

I will come to you
In your minutes and your hours
In your days and your weeks
In your months and your years
In your beginning and your end
I will come.

I will come to you
In the times of your work
In the quiet of your rest
In the laughter of your play
In your dreams and your sleep
I will come.

I will come to you
In the touch of a friend
In the caress of a lover
In the eyes of a stranger
In the smile of a child
I will come.

I will come to you
In the tears of your sorrow
In the ache of your longing
In the call of your heart
In the power of your love
I will come.

I will come to you
In the flow of your breath
In the voice of your soul
In the depth of your being
In your peace
I will come.

Beloved one
Please let me in

I Am the Reason

I am there in the Universe, I am here in your soul
For I am the reason, I am the whole.

I am there when you waken and open your eyes
For I am the reason that you can arise.
I am there in your seasons, your birth and your spring
For I am the reason behind everything.

I am there in your longing, I stir in your heart
For I am the reason, we're never apart.
I am there when you question, I am there when you call
For I am the reason, the answer to all.

I am there in your struggle, I am there in your plight
For I am the reason that knows all is right.
I am there when hope withers, and you cannot break free
For I am the reason, though you cannot see me

I am there in your courage, your strength to go on
For I am the reason, I am the one.
I am there in your turmoil, I am there in your peace
For I am the reason your heart finds release.

I am there in your summer when you flourish and bloom
For I am the reason your heart sings its tune.
I am there in your autumn when you're ripe and fulfilled
For I am the harvest, I am the yield.

I am there at your ending when your lifetime is done
For I, who so love you, then welcome you home.

Beloved Little One

GOD SPEAKING
My dear beloved little one
I give this life to you
And with this life, this gift of love
I give my blessings too
And now, beloved little one
What, on earth, will you do?

HUMAN
I will become a warrior bold,
For good and just, and right
I'll gird my loins for battle
I will not shun the fight
When love and light call out for help
To act I will not pause
I'll summon my resources
And rally to their cause.

But if, beloved little one,
Somehow along the way
You lose your strength of vision
And from this path you stray

Then how, beloved little one
Will you find your way?

My heart it will not falter
My vision will not fail
To cross this worldly ocean
I'll proudly hoist my sail.
I vow I will remember
What I have come to do
The loving beauty I come from
To that I will be true.

Ah, my dear beloved one
I wish it could be true
That it could be so easy
To do what you must do
But this journey can be perilous
And hard to travel through.

I'll fight my worldly battles
I'll not shun the inner fight
I am sure that I will triumph
And stay true to my light
But if my footsteps falter
And should my vision fail

I ask that you be there for me
If my light begins to pale.

My dear beloved little one
I am always there for you
To give you strength and courage
To help to see you through
And remember, always, little one
My blessings go with you.

Final Musings

They Told Me

They told me t'would be easy
To write my poetry
Without its rhyme, the reason why
It brings delight to me.

They told me 'tis the fashion
To write poetry this way
That needs no scan or metre
Which seems a shame, I'd say.

I really tried to write their way
I truly thought I could
Abandon rhyme, and, given time
Write poems as I should.

But rhymes, they just kept creeping in
Ignore them though I would
And, also, if I may say so
Some of them were good.

The tutor, she was not impressed
And neither were my peers
They'd cracked the art of rhyme-less verse
That pleased their modern ears.

But those darn rhymes are satisfying
I cannot let them go
So I've written this here poem
I'm a stubborn so and so.

Twenty Poems

Twenty poems partly written
Waiting for their words and rhyme
Twenty titles titivating
Nagging me to find the time
To heed their call, give them attention
To write and write and write again
Until those poems are completed
Ready then to entertain.

Twenty poems, all part written
All aspire to be complete
Twenty strong poetic babies
Trying to stand and find their feet
All eager to find expression
All eager to have their say
Each one hoping they might see
Themselves arrayed in print one day.

Nineteen poems (one's completed)
Looking enviously on
As the chosen one, perfected
Is copyrighted and then gone
All those poems, such potential

Waiting there, so hopefully
Now are joined by several others
So twenty becomes twenty-three!

Teatime

You'll have to cook the tea again
I'm busy as can be
I'm up at Gladstone's Library
Writing poetry.

You'll have to do the hoovering
I've just not had the chance
I've got so much upon my plate
The floor's not had a glance.

You'll have to get the washing in
Before the rain clouds come
Half the clothes are really yours
When all is said and done.

Please put out the rubbish
Today the bin men come
I'm busy doing other things
I'm having so much fun.

You need to get the shopping in
I've left you quite a list
I've something in my diary
That really can't be missed.

The telephone is ringing
And I know that it's for me
Answer please, tell them to wait
Until I've had my tea.

You're really my Man Friday
Not at my beck and call
But helpful, willing, caring
I hope I've said it all
Thank you

P.S. You'll have to cook the tea again…

Teatime Extra

A very British poem.

For some their evening meal is tea
For others tea's a cuppa
Taken with a piece of cake
Then later they'll have supper.
If dinner is your name for this
Your class may well be upper.

I'm a Poet

I'm a poet, now I know it
I'm a poet, don't you know
I'm a poet, now you know it
As a poet I'm doing well
I'm a poet and I know it
But will my verses ever sell?

About the Author

Kate Quartermaine was born and bred in the English Midlands. An only child and avid reader, she used to dream of living in a house surrounded by books and maybe even writing one herself. However, the big inspiration never came, and life became full of other interests.

After college, she married and moved to Chester, where business, children and family life kept her busy for some years, but then a devastating illness, ME, and her recovery, led to a new career in holistic health care, healing and energy work.

She loved working with people and is fascinated by how, as human beings, we are all so very different, yet essentially the same.

Her spiritual journey started when, as a young girl, she asked the question, "What is this God thing all about?" Lucky enough to find a teacher in her twenties, she has had a daily meditation practice ever since.

One day a few years ago, she sat down, wrote a poem, and enjoyed the process so much that she kept writing. This book is the inevitable result.

She now has three daughters, eight grandchildren and lives in the Welsh Borders with her husband and their dog Margot in a house full of books.

Connect with Kate:

Email: kateqpoetry@gmail.com
Website: katequartermaine.co.uk
Instagram: @kateqpoetry
Facebook: Kate Quartermaine poetry

About the Illustrator

Lisa Williams has been illustrating children's books for over 25 years. Inspired by the wide variety of TAUK Kids' projects, she loves helping authors bring their stories to life.

Lisa has developed a wide array of styles as she is always happy to adapt her technique to reflect what instinctively feels 'right' for each project.

Connect with Lisa:

Facebook: @lisawilliamsillustration

Acknowledgements

Heartfelt thanks to all those who read many of these poems and gave me valuable feedback, especially Ronnie Williams, Peter Jones, Kevin Mount, Maggie Knowles, Heather and Sue Elvin, and Nicki Miller.

Thanks also to my family, the TIGS and Ann Marie, Tina Symes and others who have encouraged me along the way.
Thanks to all of you who listened when I asked, "Can I read you a poem?" or even simply announced, "I've got a poem for that," and proceeded to read it aloud.

You were all very patient. I hope you were amused.

And last, but not least, a big thank you to my husband Chris, whose excellent ear was followed by equally good editorial advice, even though I might not always have taken it on board. The poem *'Teatime'* is for you.

Printed in Great Britain
by Amazon

18149907R00086